Women Born During Tornadoes

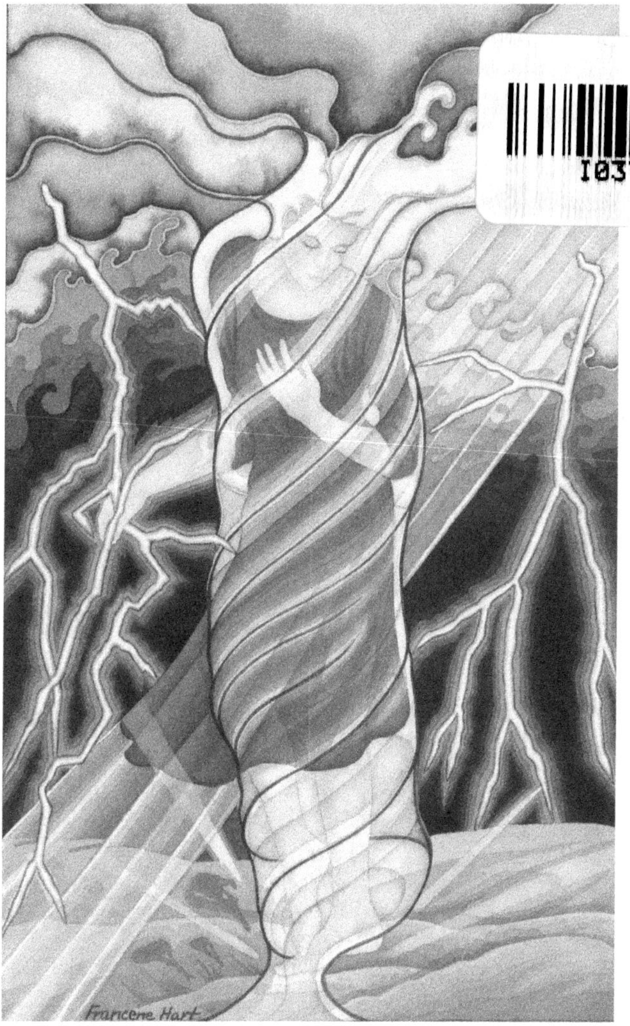

Joanne Seltzer

Plain View Press
P. O. 42255
Austin, TX 78704

plainviewpress.net
sb@plainviewpress.net
1-512-441-2452

Copyright Joanne Seltzer, 2008. All rights reserved.
ISBN: 978-1-891386-15-2
Library of Congress Number: 2008927102

Cover Art: *Tornado Dancing*, © Francene Hart.

To every woman

who is trying to make sense

of her life

and to the men

who wonder what women want

Acknowledgements

The New York State Foundation for the Arts and the Rennselaer County Council for the Arts awarded the author a Sudden Opportunity Stipend to fund the services of Kathleen Anderson, free-lance editor, who shaped a jumble of manuscripts into an orderly poetry collection. Many thanks to NYSFA, RCCA, and Kathleen Anderson for midwifing this book.

A special thank-you goes to Bill Shuff, the "computer angel" who guided a card-carrying Luddite past the many pitfalls of technology.

Another special thank-you goes to Susan Bright, publisher of Plain View Press, who sent an e-mail saying, "I like these poems." And a book was born.

Some of the poems in *Women Born During Tornadoes* first appeared, often in an earlier form, in the following publications: *Big Muddy*, "A Convoy of Headlights"; *Bird Verse Portfolios*, "Downy Woodpecker," "Mute Swans," "Prima Ballerina"; *Blueline*, "Waxwings at Ampersand"; *California State Poetry Quarterly*, "Summer Heat"; *The Cimarron Review*, "A Parable of Liberation"; *The Dekalb Literary Arts Journal*, "Forgive Us Our Trespasses"; *Earth's Daughters*, "California Water Log"; *The Glens Falls Review*, "The Sleepwalker," "Opal"; *Haight Ashbury Literary Journal*, "The Good Woman"; *Impact*, "Empty Beauty"; *The Long Story*, "A Halo for William Saad"; *The MacGuffin*, "Mohawk Music," "Old Spider Woman"; *Phoebe*, "I Can Only Advise"; *The Poet's Edge*, "Old Friend"; *Response*, "Masochist's Covenant"; *Medusa's Hairdo*, "The Legend of Chachamah"; *Samisdat*, "There Was a Day"; *Street Bagel*, "The Thursday Musical Club"; *The Third Eye*, "Buying Milk in Early December During the First Hard Snow"; *Thirteen*, "Souvenir Album"; *Waterways*, "Amber," "The Birch Tree," "The Company of Birds," "The Dryad's Story," "Fireworks," "The Fool and the Coward," "Igloo," "Illumination," "The Journey," "Pigeons," "Springtime Ceremony," "Curtain Call," "Fireworks," "Saturday Night at Bill's Café," "Morning Song," "Painted Silence."

"As the Hudson Is Swept Through the Locks" first appeared in *From the Hudson to the World: The Voices of a River*, edited by Charles Hayes (Poughkeepsie: Clearwater Sloop Restoration, Inc., 1977).

"Song of the Seeker" first appeared in *Indicting God*, edited by Paul Dilsaver (Pueblo: Academic and Arts Press, 1999).

"The Inheritance" first appeared in *Rapunzel, Rapunzel*, edited by Kathryn Machan Aal (Ithaca: McBooks Press, 1980).

"Mother's Orphan" is adapted from "A Place for Mother" which first appeared in *When I Am an Old Woman I Shall Wear Purple*, edited by Sandra Martz (Manhattan Beach: Papier Mache Press, 1987).

"The Osage River" first appeared in *Cattle Bones & Coke Machines*, edited by Dean Creighton (Maple City: Smiling Dog Press, 1995).

"Anniversary" first appeared in *Snow Summits in the Sun*, edited by Blair H. Allen (Northridge: Cerulean Press, 1988)

Contents

I

Violets	9
Women Born During Tornadoes	10
Old Spider Woman	11
The Legend of Chachamah	12
The Quilt	14
Wanda, the Cooking Teacher	16
The Thursday Musical Club	17
The Good Woman	18
Old Friend	20
I Can Only Advise	21
Empty Beauty	22
Mother's Orphan	23
The Inheritance	26

II

Mohawk Music	29
As the Hudson Is Swept Through the Locks	30
Morning Song	31
The Company of Birds	32
Waxwings at Ampersand	33
The Birch Tree	34
Global Warming	35
Summer Heat	36
Totems	38
In the Field	39
Amber	40
Wild Geese	41
Mute Swans	42
Pigeons	43
Downy Woodpecker	44
Prima Ballerina	45
Vultures of the Dead and the Living	46
The Sleepwalker	47
Travels in Missouri	48

The Osage River	49
A Convoy of Headlights	50
Saturday Night at Bill's Café	51
California Water Log	52

III

Spiritual Influences	55
Igloo	57
The Chase	58
Sailors	59
The Dryad's Story	60
A Casual Ghost	61
A Parable of Liberation	62
A Halo for William Saad	63
The Fool and the Coward	64
The Journey	65
Opal	66
Springtime Ceremony	67
Painted Silence	68
Curtain Call	69
Song of the Seeker	70
Monogamy	71
Forgive Us Our Trespasses	72
Masochist's Covenant	73
Anniversary	74
Souvenir Album	75
Buying Milk in Early December During the First Hard Snow	76
There Was a Day	77
Illumination	78
Fireworks	79
Afterword	81
About the Author	83

I

Violets

1
When I transplanted a pair of violets
to my rock garden, one a subtle white,
the other darkened by the rich pigment
that gives its name to the prism's shortest ray
neighbors laughed at me, said I'd be sorry.
I was a novice then, ignorant of
weeds and their growth: rapid, luxuriant,
hyperactive as cancer cells, wild.
I brought a few more violets from the field,
cared for them as I would
an endangered lady's-slipper
improperly taken out of nature.

2
Time fades, forms a prism
of expectations that diffract like colors.
We reach out for the object of desire
only to find that once the object is ours
we don't need it, don't want it anymore.
Nothing survived one snowless January
except the purple violets,
the white went the way of the bleeding heart.

Women Born During Tornadoes

Women born during tornadoes
carry wildness within them
that men find irresistible.

Fickle, temperamental, unable
to settle into strong relationships
or go from entry level to career
they blame unlucky parents
who blame themselves, wonder what
went wrong.

Women born during tornadoes
ghost autobiographies,
itemize devastation.
They get shot by boyfriends' wives
and confess to other women's fantasies.

They are forgiven, then go home again
to heal and borrow money
they can't or don't or won't repay.

Old Spider Woman

This lovely land was formed by the spirit
called Old Spider Woman or Thought Woman.
By thinking she created the world.
But is she proud of her creation?

She is known for the tobacco men smoke,
for the corn women grind into grits,
for the power engendered when
this lovely land was formed by the spirit.

Sometimes her people forget
how dark the world before she began
giving birth to new gods.

Thought Woman dwells in everyone
from the Abenaki to the Tlingit,
in places holy and profane.

She is proud of animals and inanimate things,
of the constantly changing heaven,
of the milk-fog that flows from her breast.

But what will become of sun and moon
when no one is left to study the sky,
when Old Spider Woman looks at her land
and is no longer proud?

The Legend of Chachamah

1
Chachamah throws her teeth
to the young women
who form a circle,

the bright, broken
remnants
of the Shekinah,

who let the teeth fall
at their feet
like a bridal bouquet.

2
She has no speech
no hair
and leans on a cane

wearing foreskin
for a wedding band
stars for fingernails

and instead of eyes
two chunks
of precious topaz.

3
She has two old chairs,
one for herself
and one for her life.

Soon
she will need just one –
not for sitting

but for fire
that gives the Inquisitor
pleasure.

The Quilt

1
I pause before the quilt
upon the wall
of the vestibule
in my house of worship
created
by the fervent fingers
of many women
each of whom contributed
a square or two
a stitch or two
a printout of the soul
knowing she would remain
as women have always been
anonymous.

2
There is something
ecumenical
about a quilt.

It has no verbal language
no prejudice
no guile.

Its sheer existence
is proof of the potential
every woman has
to be something more.

Some women quilt
while at prayer.

3
Inside the sanctuary
of worship
I tell myself silently,
"Whatsoever a woman sews,
that shall she also reap."

In time the quilt will crumble
into particles of dust
by the same process
that brings facelessness
to cadavers
which does not prove
that the work was not sacred,
nor that quilters
are not immortal.

Wanda, the Cooking Teacher

She spies on her ingredients
from daydream to acquisition
to assembly to storage,
slits carrots' throats on the diagonal,
drains beets' blood into a blue coffin.
After flaying two Bermuda onions
she blows her nose, blaming
chocolate kisses that served as lunch
thanks to her husband
who enters the home classroom
flourishing a spring bouquet
enhanced by a smooch
then helps himself to squash crème soup,
broccoli floret sauté,
braised tempeh atop a millet bed
and raspberry delight.

The Thursday Musical Club

The Thursday morning lady singers,
silk fingers folded over uplifted breasts,
appear on stage at a college ballroom
for a concert of Brahms' and Gershwin's best.

In gowns of satin and organdy film,
adorned with smiles of chiffon and lace,
an earring enhancing each waxen lobe,
the mannequins show their harmonious face.

Traditional female choral airs
rehearsed in spring like a schoolgirl's lesson
are sung by clusters of primrose voices
even if the "Summertime" of Bess
is out of season.

After gracious bows to soft applause
allowing themselves the lifting of skirts
the letting out of bone-caught breath
those Thursday women stumble down
Friday's pirate plank
into an ocean of raucous harpies.

The Good Woman

1
The dirt waits
for her to push, scrub
and curse it away.

For seven years
she has been energizing
my house,

telling me about
the old country,
the Ukraine,

spitting out venom
over her ex-daughter-in-law,
the topless dancer,

scolding the child
she brings with her,
a redheaded little girl

that her son
dumped upon her.

Invoking God
all the time she is
polishing,

she warns the child
to drink her milk.

When her work is done
she gathers the day's wages
and the child.

2
In the old country
the Communists ruined her life,
then Hitler—

she was thrown
out of her home in winter,
taken by boxcar
to a German slave factory
as a young girl

and lived in France
after the war.
Now she's an American.

Having lost
both health and beauty
she hopes someday

that someone will write
this epitaph:
Here Lies a Good Woman.

Old Friend

Ages ago your first letter
memorable as a girl's menarche
came to me unsolicited
from another coast, spitting complaints
about the treacherous battlefield
in that private war called family
we standard-bearers refuse to quit.

You spat invectives
at the conventional life you lead
and pressed your spit like roses
between the leaves of softcover books.

Women taught us discontent. Lilith.
Vashti, first wife of Esther's king.
Morgan le Fay and Vivian.
The puppeteer's belligerent Judy.

But when I visited your distant place
after years of letters, years of silence,
your tremulous voice railed at nothing but
the barking dog you put outside.
This, then, is the word made flesh
with all the public parts concealed.

I Can Only Advise

you must make your own decision
to report or not report
the incident

don't shower   don't change
your clothes   don't comb your hair
we must confirm the accusation
has your father done this
before   did your mother try
to stop him

you shouldn't have left the tavern
with a stranger   did you flirt
did he menace with a knife
or just a penis   did he hurt
your throat

should you tell your husband
your boyfriend
you must make your own decision
I don't know your husband
your boyfriend   I can only advise

against gonorrhea

those cigarette burns on your vulva
will heal   no one will notice
the scars

Empty Beauty

I was a child who cared only for books
but lived in a house of knickknacks.
I despised my mother's curio shelf:
the crystal, silver, porcelain objects.

At college I learned the beauty of art
by hanging defiant sun-like objects
next to pink oleanders above my bookshelf.

After my marriage I bought a cabinet
right out of *Better Homes*. The huge,
mahogany piece featured many new objects
including my latest literature: cookbooks
and Dr. Spock. One day, a pair of vases
came to me from my mother.

My mother explained: "Too many possessions
collect dust on my curio shelf.
Please accept these Baccarat vases
with delicate bubbles of handblown beauty
like the glass in old French books.
Your house could use a few fine things."

Slowly my house began to fill
with my mother's dispossessions
to which I added a Steuben urn.
I stopped buying books.
The Subject Was Roses has given way to vases
empty of beauty

and something in me violently objects
to what I am: a library of transparent books,
a brittle grouping off the shelf.

Mother's Orphan

1
Ask her what she wants.
If she doesn't know
ask her if she's happy.
If she says she isn't
ask what will make her happy.
She will either say
she doesn't know
or she will be silent.
Tell her how much you love her.
Promise you won't forsake her.

2
Place One has an eight-year waiting list.
Place Two has a nursing home odor.
Place Three is in a bad neighborhood.
Place Four is in another city.
Place Five won't take Medicaid.
Place Six takes only terminal cases.
Place Seven doesn't offer therapy.
Place Eight puts three in a room.
Place Nine requires a hike to the dining room.
Place Ten demands Mother's money up front.
Place Eleven decides Mother won't fit in.

3
Though Mother says
she doesn't belong anywhere
you keep on looking.

You learn about levels of care,
levels of caring.

The Jewish Home offers
a night in the Rabbi's room
when the Rabbi isn't there

to newly matched couples
who hanker after
geriatric sex.

4
While you ponder your choices
Mother continues to slip.

She thinks she will go to jail
for being a dope addict.

She thinks there's a conspiracy
against the family.

She worries about the poison
in the drinking water.

Though people call her *lady*
she isn't sure if she's a woman
or a man.

5
There's no umbrella now
to separate you
from eternity.

Meanwhile an army
marches behind you
in the rain.

Your friends are dead
or dying.

You're a survivor
with all the loneliness
of survivorship.

6
My hair has turned white.
My skin is parchment.
I have a bulldog's jowls.

I ask myself
what Mother's face is doing
in the mirror.

She sticks out her tongue.

The Inheritance

I've learned to accept the medical diagnosis:
female pattern alopecia, a hereditary disorder.

If I live to marvel at my eightieth birthday
baby-pink scalp will shine shamelessly
through silky strands of fine white hair.

But if passing years can somehow transform me
into a woman worn bald with wisdom,
dignified and lovable despite eccentricity,
I'll proudly wear my glossy-headed legacy
in memory of my maternal grandmother.

Born to an age of braids and ribbons,
afflicted in every bone of her skull
by the pain of Victorian women,
my grandmother combed and knotted her losses.

II

Mohawk Music

The river
has always been here.
Long before the ditch was dug
mostly by Irish and Italian labor
fresh mountain water
ambled toward the ocean
through the lands of the Five Nations.
The birds sang in woodland chorus.

Cows came to the fields
brought by the farmers
who settled the valley
where the drums no longer beat.
They lowed to the morning
with the wakening birds
and the farmers heard
a duet of river music.

Mules pulled heavy barges
bearing machinery
lumber and iron ore
along the muddy towpaths.
On chilly mornings in warm-weather months
bargemen blew
the horns of the river
that beckoned the birds and the cows.

When cities broke the lines on maps
the farmers planted houses.
Once at daybreak as the fog rolled deep
I heard a foghorn bellow
like a bovine protesting,
defining, delimiting
the river.

As the Hudson Is Swept Through the Locks

my river
which once boasted
of clean Adirondack waters
has been defiled
while descending
southward to the ocean

my river
is now polluted
by pebbles grated against
a ruthless current

long ago
it left the rarefied
mountain air
to move within
a middling valley,
soon it will pass
through the final gate
of the barge canal
surging toward low tide
at sea

a lonely drop
will disappear
into the ocean
with infinite sadness
and no ghost dance
can halt the flow
or send my river backward
to its source

Morning Song

Do I hear
oriental music?
A bird
has brought me out of sleep
before the devil could make
his morning round.

But the song I hear
is not some wild bird
who doesn't care
if the world wakes up,

it is a prisoner
gone mad,
banging her head
against a window, thinking
she has found infinity.

The Company of Birds

1
Last week the birds turned frantic
in the meadow.
I saw a sun-splashed warbler
among excited sparrows.
The butterfly gave innocence
to the company of birds.

2
Two ragged silhouettes
fly north against the weather.
All the birdsong gone,
the butterfly beats her fatal wings.

3
One robin
snared in flight by an iron fence
dangles from the mesh.

4
Behind the Friendly Restaurant
vintage rock-'n'-roll
blares from a pickup truck
at the young scarecrow
who rakes the autumn trash.

Waxwings at Ampersand

Wild roses fade quickly in summer
in spite of barricade by thorn,
thicket and bumblebee. No mere
mortal soars without feathers torn
or tearing, turning heads that remember
the tale of man's ineptitude.
In God's dark December
not even Indian craft found food
up this peak of Stone Age ice
and Hell's molt. We're not born twice,
will never tread air, for Paradise
is Earth where cedar waxwings play.
A child screams. God looks away.
The pale sun flaunts malignant rays.

The Birch Tree

Ancient mountains
grew weary of my humanity,
induced me to make love to a birch tree.

It was an act without commitment,
yet I put up with the peeling skin
that other women find repulsive.

I begged, then, for absolution
from the sin of the greenhouse effect
and the transgression of acid rain.

However personified, a tree
remains the tortuous symbol of
the cross and immortality.

Though trees can sing, mine became silent.

Global Warming

We are lost: everywhere
carbon dioxide
dilutes fresh air.

The ocean pushes
as if with child
across the world's beaches.

Islands disappear
like Atlantis, engulfed
by melted glaciers.

Starving children watch
holding hands
while the fierce water witch

devours gingerbread
and legend.

Summer Heat

summer heat
steamed up
all morning

rising
from the valley

touching even
the northern
mountains

        cloudless
              cruel
        afternoon

the twilight sky
turned
prematurely black

lightning broke
in the river

followed by
rumbles
of thunder

        then fire
            & water
      exploded together

the wind passed
limply
toward the ocean

& evening air
hung heavy

like a woman
in her nightgown
brooding

Totems

If people are walking trees
as it is said
we haul heavy totems,
call them backbones.

Hair is a clump of leaves.
Arms are swinging branches.
Legs are displaced roots.
Sex organs are sex organs.

The acorns
we drop on the ground
grow up to imitate
our sighs.

To wooden things like us
war is a forest fire
burning, burning, burning
out of control.

In the Field

Eyes form a camera
in which images
are recorded

such as the male goldfinch
who poses
on a cone of ripe sumac,

black-capped energy
above
the color of dried blood,

not a composition
created by
conventional wisdom

but the journeywork
of an intelligence
that knows

minor art
can be mistaken.

Amber

I will find my way to the cradle
of the runic northern word
and comb the beach near Klaipeda
from twilight till dawn
looking for solid sunlight
cast ashore from the Baltic Sea
by dead Lithuanian gods.

Gulls will sweep like ancient tribes
up and down the sky
as I sift the sand for a piece of mist,
an antiquarian fern,
the tomb of an insect long extinct
to set in an amulet for warmth
against the arctic noon.

Wild Geese

1
A wild goose spreads his wings
in the Norman's Kill,
his mate can only stare
at her reflection,
both of them caught
by the encroaching ice.

2
We leap from year to year,
from one war to another,
from love to abuse.
Are we different from
wild geese
who respond without thinking,
who are trapped in our shared
environment?

Mute Swans

White necks
curve gracefully
into an S

as they hiss
and grunt
in spite of their beauty

or give loud
trumpet calls
that are seldom heard.

Yeats immortalized
a whole flock of them
at Coole

but only one
became Zeus
of the great wings

who opened his black-
and-orange beak
to announce

that nothing
creates more sadness
or distress

than complete
satisfaction.

Pigeons

In my childhood ghetto
the pigeons
seemed like family,
billing and cooing
and bobbing their heads.

I call them
the power
of sublimation,

a reminder
of how much easier
outgrowing childhood is
than escaping it.

Downy Woodpecker

If you could comprehend
the laws of gravity
you would tumble
to the ground
instead of creeping
on the underside
of that branch,

you would exchange
your outlaw's mask
for something
more conventional
such as a blank stare.

But you don't know
the rules
nor understand
the resolute nature
of gravity
and behavior.

Prima Ballerina

Small to the point
of dwarfdom,
the ruby-throated
hummingbird
whirls so intensely
that her feathers
dissolve into
one luminous green glow
that moves forward now
and backward

She has come
in one lifetime
from a humble home
of leaf down
on spidersilk
to this great theater
with its trumpetry,
its fame
and crimson flowers

Though she will be
in the limelight
for only the time
her body stays young,
her admirers
will remember
ephemeral things,
manifestations
of eternal movement

Vultures of the Dead and the Living

1
Humbling herself
through carrion
she keeps the planet clean

and symbolizes
the guardian angel
known as Mother Nature.

For example,
Parsees of India
do not bury their dead,

they hang them
on iron gratings
in towers of silence.

2
They roost.
They soar.
They purify the dead

while flesh becomes food
and humans
prey upon life itself.

Their greed
has no spiritual
signification.

The Sleepwalker

During nature's most enduring trance
a massive grizzly emerges from his den.
Some fanciful sting or intrusive wind
ruffled his blanket of hibernation.

The flat-footed form lumbers through midnight
without blinking diffident eyes,
deepset in a face without expression.
Head bent forward, the gruff voice grunts.

If he encounters people in the dark
he ignores our frantic, screaming questions.
The bear is breathing deeply.
Quick, out of his path
before teeth and claws strike murder
disconnected from the brain.

After the prowl across white territory
pilot feet return to the comfort of the lair.
But talonprints will linger past the dawn
like black dreams etched in melting snow.

Travels in Missouri

To experience a place
you have to make a commitment
of one complete moon.

You will witness the obese moon,
the anorectic moon,
the agoraphobic moon.

When you and the moon
do a belly dance
she will wave her purple cloud
through your red silk scarf
of earth's expression.

The Osage River

Engineers, designing for power,
sized her up, surrounded her,
called her the Missouri whore.

Snorting at impassive men,
she wipes the foam from her mouth,
pulls herself together,
a gentle spirit cursing God,

then travels east, as always,
toward the Missouri.

A Convoy of Headlights

The karma of a place
includes its funerals.

The long procession
led by a police car
shows the world someone was loved
by townsfolk who follow
the somber limousine
gone carefully past
a hiker with bleeding feet.

Afraid fate will punish you
for trying to envision
the home of the soul
that levitates now
in the bright Missouri sky
you tell yourself this
would be a lovely town to die in.

The funerals of a place
project its karma.

Saturday Night at Bill's Café

Macks Creek, Missouri

I marveled at Bill
the barefoot owner
and his chorus-girl wife,
thinking this is what genuine
hillbillies look like
until the waitress
feather in her headband
finally took my order.

His ragged overalls
about to pop
Bill danced with his wife
then whirled a few
hillbilly ladies
along the aisles between
communal tables.

The wife passed a cup
for local talent
that made the music alcove jump:
banjo strummer,
pair of guitars,
Hank Williams imitation,
old man drumming
a set of dry cow bones.

Cowboys were there
and colonial women
and a hand-holding pair
of bright crayolas,
even Minnie Mouse
wearing a polka-dot dress
cool for a late October night.

California Water Log

San Diego. Water served only by request
in every restaurant, including Anthony's
which offers french fries or pilaf with dinner,
then bilks me of 75¢ for a baked potato.
At the waterfront a homeless young man
begs carfare to the VA hospital,
slinks away like one of the zoo's great cats.

San Luis Obispo. With Swiss-Italian abandon
the Madonna Inn sells water by the night,
but I freeload off Cousin Betty's
scant ration that she shares with tuberous begonias
and red peppers foraged by deer.
I promise to wash my hair in Cambria.

San Simeon. No water flows in the castle
Hearst devoted decades to unbuilding.
Cary Grant, playing the favorite guest,
in deadpan called this a splendid place
for an unemployed actor to spend the Depression.

Monterey. Shops have taken over Cannery Row
where Steinbeck's books provide local color
alongside wearable interpretations of
sea lion, sea otter, dolphin, seal and whale.
At the aquarium a well-fed shark
shares the mock ocean with selected fish.
Why the sardine stopped coming nobody knows.

III

Spiritual Influences

1
Immerse yourself in me:
the stuff you were conceived of,
that cushioned you
before you were born,
that John the Baptist
sprinkled upon bent heads,
that you now imbibe
and excrete.

You are water too.
You flow.
You freeze.
You build a dam.
You thaw.
You are blocked by ice.
Ice jams beget floods.

2
God created the flood
before the rainbow.
If I were not water
I would choose to be the dove,
circling above
my own reflection
looking for peace.
If I found an olive branch
I would offer it for shelter
within your cupped hands.

3
My sins wash away
through storm sewers
that symbolize
the blocked bowel
of suburbia.

But when I walk in the rain
I remember
God is infinite water.

Even the rainbow
reminds me
of all your broken promises,
pear-shaped units of water,
the indefinite mist
we aspire to become.

Igloo

I touch the hand
of a sleeping man
who reminds me of
another man
whom I targeted for transport
to some invented land
where a woman and man
can freely experience the night.

Yupik hospitality:
sharing a cozy wife
with a stranger.

The Chase

He is following me again.
I thought I had shaken him
but I sense a stalking presence
behind my left shoulder.

I stoop and gather a handful of dust
to throw backward into his hooded face.
Slits shut from the macelike sting.

I prolong the chase from my father's grave
to a northern land of peaks and dips
where among the alpine lakes
I simulate my mother's wedding dance
until I am isolated on
some ledge above the water
where no handful of dust can be found.

With one arm around my shoulder
he will raise his grim hood,
place his cheek against mine.

At last we will share one shadow,
the touch of our first dry kiss.

Sailors

I never could say no
to a sailor

nor can I remember
faces, voices

or personalities
but only the touch

of multiple fingers
rubbing themselves

against me
before plunging

naked into my deep
then pulling out

disappearing
except those few

whom I keep for my own
satisfaction,

my own precious bones
culled from the ocean's debris.

The Dryad's Story

Everything was brown.

As I drew my fluttering veils
afraid
yet somewhat brave
a young man
entered my fantasy
beneath the acorn tree.

We kissed.

"I'm too old for you," I said,
"go home to your wife
and children."

I'm as old as civilization.

He went home like a myth
to his cottage near the ocean.

Civilization decays.

I draw my fluttering veils
toughened by the knowledge
that I won't grow old
as quickly
as a young man with a family
covered by coarse sand.

A Casual Ghost

Little man,
as we rode the dome car
from Denali Park
to Anchorage
I pointed at a bull moose
drinking of wilderness.

In return
you found me a slice
of mountain
afloat between dense clouds
and spoke about
your long-dead wife
and your suede hat
covered with souvenir pins
from all the trips taken
without her.

You ordered beer
and more beer
and you laughed
and you laughed.

Little man
with a huge camera case
a hat heavy with pins
a thick German accent
and a missing right thumb,
my face now haunts
your album
along with many other
strange and
familiar ghosts.

A Parable of Liberation

Long after hope was abandoned
for my rescue from the dark turret
I met an errant knight
riding his horse through town.

Words of felicity
flowed through his headpiece:
he thought me a beauty
in the lamplight glow.

I listened to his love-talk
courteously spoken
but he sped to a different quest
before I could question him further.

A Halo for William Saad

This man—a Christian Arab—wore a halo
for six postsurgical weeks.
The device was joined to his head
by the hammers of skilled medical carpenters
who drove four spiral nails
above the four corners of his brain.
Blood oozed from four neat holes.
The steel rim was held by a pink plastic vest
lined with fluffy lambswool
and trussed down the back to extend
the man's embroidered seam.
Whenever a nail worked loose
it was pulled from soggy bone
by the pliers of skilled medical carpenters
and replaced.
The diabolical spacesuit
medieval in its modernity
is healing the man's vulnerable spine,
suffering inside his circular glow
a fusion of bone on bone
or the rising of the man's spirit
through the letting of his blood.

The Fool and the Coward

don't call me a coward
you know I would have gone with you
for a flight in your pickup truck

>you would spread
>your Persian rug
>on the floor
>beneath the dash

but after I said yes
and chose a quiet meeting place
you changed your mind

>you would hover
>with your carpet
>above the interstate
>toll free

so don't call me a coward
dear coward
call me a fool

The Journey

Holding close to yesterday's embrace
I feel the warm and slightly tonic fluids
that comfort body and soul
and give me strength for the journey.

It's lucky to be born with a caul
but luckier still to break one
(let no one say a battered woman
can't leave home).

Life is the search for a door
that flies open. In the sky
the devil's giant shekel shines.

Opal

I wear him on my finger knowing
he is the patron of evil
lifted from the ground.

My lover is unlucky.
My lover is semiprecious.
I enjoy twisting my hand to watch him reflect

the sky,
the sea,
the craft of hand-wrought gold.

I have learned to ignore the deadly flaw:
a cold horizon that separates ocean from air.

Springtime Ceremony

We entered the garden through hallowed gates,
fingers interlaced.

While the wind intoned a plaintive song
flanked by rows of weathered stone
we moved along the aisle.

Sipping sweet saliva wine
we pledged abortion for our infant devotion.

Straight poplars attended
our shadowy bed between fir-green mounds.
I lay upon my lover's black raincoat.
He lay upon my pale sheath.
His tenor manhood smashed a high-pitched glass,

as the spirits applauded, trapped
inside those hallowed gates.

Painted Silence

Mint-julep cool as melting snow,
has a nap to it—the velvet
fingered by a painter newly blind.
It hovers like incense
at a Greek mass for the dead.

I didn't invite but when it came
offered a cup of herbal tea.
I looked at it and it looked at me,
two strangers with the same destiny
filling the dark hollows of my bed.

Curtain Call

Don't feel cheated
when I tell you
this is a one-act play.

You expected
five, or at least three,
Shakespearean segments
but now the curtain
flutters down
and the lights flicker on.

You recognize
the shabbiness of
your own reality.

Song of the Seeker

Sometimes at night I lie in bed pleading
for thunder or vision, for your voice
as you invent excuses without heeding
my prayers, my supplications, my cries.
Impatient and alone my soul is bleeding.

Other nights you lose most of your power
as I embrace the living Buddha
or drift away into Tao
or pierce the gentle womb of Great Mother.
You said, "I am your God, there is no other."
I shaved my head, became your bride.
Husband, your touch leaves me unsatisfied:
to grow I need a variety of lovers.

Monogamy

No red roses. No helium balloons.
No card. No gift. No kiss. No sex.
No party. No new vows. No love you.

Up ahead the Promised Land beckons.
But not to us. We live
in the sterile desert we call home.

Most of our friends have died or fallen
into the idolatry of Me.
We still pretend to be a couple,

though one of our wedding bands (yours)
was stolen many years ago
and the other (mine) sits in the vault.

We both know this won't last forever.
The survivor will drink the champagne.

Forgive Us Our Trespasses

Strange dreams threaten fire
in decaying hostels
where dark, hay-covered lofts
harbor vermin.

I touch my face
to the choleraic pillow
where someone has already slept,
go tranquil and awaken
choking from the heavy warmth
of my husband
forgiving my trespasses.

Masochist's Covenant

To formalize our relationship
we signed a covenant in early history
that bound us together eternally
with Promethean chains.

After the honeymoon rape,
he begat & begat & begat.

We wandered from place to place.
In the cities—humiliation.
In the villages—torment.
In the faraway campsites—savagery.

Our depraved desire was gratified
by a closet of whipcords & shackles.

I ignored the frantic warnings:
"He'll cut you too deeply & kill you
or force you to turn the knife against him.
Cast him off & take a gentle partner."

I savored those pleasurable pinpricks.
He adored my high-pitched screams.

Each year we set an anniversary table
& tell the children about our wedding.
We all stand up while an open door reveals
a goblet of wine, never emptied.

Anniversary

Before each anniversary
comes the calm.
We light one candle
and snuff it out in memory
of progress. No solutions
exist—only a number of watts
per hour. Social revolutions
grow from such disharmony
mimicking our most important
product. Quarrels come
and go like electricity—
wasteful and brilliant.

Souvenir Album

stains from yellowed orchids
   watermark
my memory pages

the endpapers are roughened
   by the grit
of careless erasures

a naked body centerfold
   reclines
between hidebound covers

flattened, pressed
   under a stack
of weighted years

Buying Milk in Early December During the First Hard Snow

I watch the early morning boys
with tight crotched blue jeans
blond & dark faces

my fingers threaten
to touch their crusted beards
my gut muscles tighten

>   I am corrupted by
>   a long & comfortable marriage
>   I scatter in the street

the boys notice the hard snow
sometimes they stop & stare
often they turn away

discomfited by winter eyes
hair blown to the wind
a body that bends with fantasy

>   me & one of those morning boys
>   one day holding hands
>   over a quart of milk

but the snowfall deepens
in upstate New York
as our days grow darkly short

There Was a Day

when the jagged parts of my life
came together
like a jigsaw puzzle
with key pieces missing

I was tempted to follow
the enigma
over the jigsaw's edge
to a place where no one knew my name

but I put on my best
medieval smile
after carefully combing my hair
and walked proudly into town

so the world could see my face
radiant from dishonor

Illumination

no need for chandeliers
or sconces
where art glows like
a divine spark

no need to explain
shadow images
in this observatory
we call
the real world

face to face with God,
heaven
teases us with darkness
by stretching
beyond our vision

Fireworks

Watch from your back porch
during a heat wave in May
with your hair hanging wet
and your partner beside you
gently rubbing your shoulder
while you chew a dried peach.

Pinwheels, Roman candles, rockets.

Though you can hardly see
the patterns through the trees
you hear explosive
red   white   pink   yellow   blue
and know that fireworks display
both war and peace.

Yellow sand, verdigris
charcoal, nitre, sulfur
benzoine, camphor
zinc, iron, steel, copper
lampblack, gunpowder.

In the last burst of love enjoy
the last burst of color.

Afterword

Certain poems in this collection were written during the off years of a long, fulfilling marriage and express emotions banished abruptly when my husband began his unwinnable fight against the illnesses that would kill him. But art has a life of its own! My "anti-marriage poems" are offered as a testimonial to the commitment that keeps family together in times of crisis, discord, triviality, and ennui.

When turbulence ends, boredom becomes a blessing.

About the Author

Joanne Seltzer was born in Detroit but has lived in upstate New York long enough to call it home. Hundreds of her poems have appeared in a variety of journals and anthologies, and she has published three small press poetry chapbooks. Some of her poems have been set to music, some used as classroom texts. She has served as a contest judge.

Seltzer's first true poem, "Dreamland," was written at the age of seven and published the next year in *Children's Playmate Magazine*. After many years of estrangement, she and her muse reconnected with an art form built of dreams.

Author photo by Bob Woll.

www.ingramcontent.com/pod-product-compliance
Lightning Source LLC
Chambersburg PA
CBHW071028080526
44587CB00015B/2540